All Wrapped Up

by

Helen Orme

Rans☺m

All Wrapped Up
by Helen Orme
Illustrated by Chris Askham

Published by Ransom Publishing Ltd.
Radley House, 8 St. Cross Road, Winchester, Hampshire SO23 9HX, UK
www.ransom.co.uk

ISBN   978 184167 150 5
First published in 2013
Copyright © 2013 Ransom Publishing Ltd.

Illustrations copyright © 2013 Chris Askham

A CIP catalogue record of this book is available from the British Library.

Siti Musa

Wall · Photos · Friends

Hi! I'm Siti Musa.

Siti is a Swahili (African) name meaning 'Lady'.

I'm the oldest in my family. I have two brothers, Daudi and Hanif, and a kid sister Afia.

My dad is a deputy head at our school, which can be bad news sometimes!

My mum is a social worker.

Lu Clarke

Wall · Photos · Friends

I'm Lu Clarke and I'm an only child. My dad is a businessman – he has an IT office in the town centre. My mum, who is Chinese, works in a bank.

My mum's parents (Po-po and Gong-gong – our name for grandparents) live by the sea. They used to have a Chinese restaurant and my mum worked there when she was younger. My other grandparents live close to us.

My parents want the best for me – but they don't always ask me what *I* want.

Kelly Jonson

Wall · Photos · Friends

I'm Kelly Jonson.

My mum is a single parent. She works as a solicitor. I've got an older brother, Jamie. His girlfriend is Susie.

My parents split when I was very young, and Dad remarried. We don't have any contact with Dad and his new family.

I really want to be a writer – oh, and I fancy Gary! I've decided that I want to be a vegetarian.

Rachel Phillips

Wall · Photos · Friends

I'm Rachel Phillips.

My parents split about 4 years ago. Dad runs a small printing business, and Mum is office manager at our school.

I live with Mum and spend weekends with Dad. His new wife is Janine. They have two young children, a boy and a new baby girl. It's O.K. visiting them, but I'd rather be with Mum.

My older brother Wil is at sixth-form college.

Donna Mills

Wall · Photos · Friends

I'm Donna Mills.

My dad's a bus driver and my mum works in a shop.

I have two older sisters, Marie and Briony. Marie's friend Susie is Kelly's brother's girlfriend.

My brother, Michael, is the youngest.

I love animals and going swimming.

There isn't much spare cash in our family – which makes things hard sometimes.

Chapter
1

Siti and Donna walked into their form room. Kathryn Mason was talking.

' … and I'm going to get a new phone. It's top of the range – it … '

'I'm fed up with her and her Christmas presents!' said Donna.

Kathryn heard her.

'I suppose you won't get much,' she said to Donna. She knew Donna's family hadn't got much money to spare. 'Maybe a new school bag.'

She looked at Siti. 'I don't suppose you'll get anything either. You don't do Christmas, do you?'

That made Siti cross.

'You don't know anything, do you? Anyway, my dad says Christmas isn't just about religion any more. It's a winter festival as well and he doesn't see why we can't all enjoy it.'

It wasn't like Siti to get wound up. Rachel, Kelly and Lu hurried over.

'Do you remember when we were in infant school?' asked Lu. 'And our teacher wouldn't let Siti be in the Christmas play?'

'She cried all the way home,' said Rachel. 'So her mum came in and said she had to be in it.'

Donna laughed. 'I remember. They made her an angel and the rest of us just got to be the sheep.'

'You still follow her like sheep.' That was Kathryn. She had to have the last word.

Chapter

2

_____

'What are we going to do about presents?' asked Kelly. She wanted to stop Siti thinking about Kathryn.

'It will cost a lot,' said Donna. 'And I've got all my family to buy for.' She looked worried.

They looked at Siti. She always had good ideas.

'I know,' she said. 'We can *make* presents.'

'But I can't make things. Can't I just buy you each something?' That was Lu. She didn't have any brothers or sisters to buy for.

'No,' said Siti. 'If we do it, we *all* do it.'

'I think it's a great idea,' said Kelly. 'What sort of things can we make?'

'I'll make sweets for everyone,' decided Siti.

Rachel was thinking hard. 'I know,' she said, 'but I'm not telling.'

'We'll all have to keep it a secret,' said Kelly. 'Or it won't be a surprise.'

Chapter
3

Lu moaned to Kelly. 'What are you going to do?' she asked. 'I can't think of anything.'

'I know what I'm doing,' said Kelly. 'You can help me if you like.'

'But I can't do anything.'

'Yes you can.' She told Lu about her idea. Lu thought it was great. She loved stuff like that.

'Yes, O.K., I'll help.'

Donna was still thinking. She didn't moan, but she really couldn't think what she was going to do.

* * * * *

Donna was sitting in the form room by herself. Mrs Morgan came in. She looked at Donna.

'Are you all right?'

Donna shrugged.

'Come and help me then, and you can
tell me all about it, if you like.'

Mrs Morgan was busy sorting out odd ends of cotton and material. Donna enjoyed her lessons, and she was happy to help. She told Mrs Morgan about Siti's idea.

'But they all have things they're good at,' said Donna. 'I can't think of anything!'

'You're good at textiles. Why don't you make gifts from this scrap stuff? You can work in here and use up whatever you want.'

Chapter
4

When Donna got into school the next day, she went straight to Mrs Morgan.

'I'm going to make mascots for their school bags.' She looked at her teacher. 'Do you have any buttons or sequins and things I could use?'

'I've got a few things,' she said. 'But you mustn't use new stuff. That costs me money!'

Donna started work that lunch-time. She told the others she was working on their presents, but that was all she told

them. Mrs Morgan let her into the textiles room and even hid her behind a notice board.

She had worked out a different thing for each of her friends. Siti was to get a mouse;

Kelly a fluffy dog, Lu could have a cat and Rachel a giraffe.

She hunted through the bits of material until she found just the right bits. She'd get these done and then she could make more for her real sisters. She wasn't sure about her brother, Michael, though. He wasn't really into fluffy stuff.

She went every lunch-time for the rest of the week and had finished two and started a third, but then something awful happened.

She was found out!

Chapter
5

She thought it was Siti and the others, but then she recognised the voices. It was all right, it was Sally and Hannah, and the new girl Megan.

Sally put her head round the notice board.

'Hi,' she said. 'What are you up to?'

Then Hannah noticed the finished ones. 'Hey, these are good. What are they for?'

'Christmas presents.'

'Cool. Hey, will you make one for me? I'll pay you for it.'

Donna thought about it. She'd still have time to make more.

'O.K.' she agreed. 'But don't tell Siti or the others, or it won't be a surprise.'

* * * * *

Then it got mad! Sally didn't tell Siti, but she did show some of the other girls. Everybody wanted one. Donna was working all the time. She even took stuff home. It was lucky Marie and Briony were out a lot. But she was earning loads of money. She might even be able to buy presents for them all.

Frankie was just handing over her money when Mrs Morgan came in.

'What's going on here? Donna, I'm really disappointed in you.'

She had a real go at Donna.

Donna burst into tears.

'I couldn't help it,' she sobbed.

'Well, you can give all the money you got to my Charity Box.'

'But I won't be able to get any presents for anyone now.'

Mrs Morgan was cross, but as she calmed down she began to feel sorry for Donna.

'O.K.,' she said. 'Here's the deal. You can keep half the money, for presents.

'As long as you make a mascot for me.'

Siti's Sisters
The early years

– one year on:
the Sisters
are older

Brother Bother
Illustrated by Cathy Brett

Horsing Around
Illustrated by Cathy Brett

New Man
Illustrated by Cathy Brett

Who's Who
Illustrated by Cathy Brett

Wet!
Illustrated by Cathy Brett

Moving
Illustrated by Cathy Brett

– another year on:
The Sisters have grown up (well, nearly ...)

Party Time
Illustrated by Chris Askham

She's My Friend Now
Illustrated by Chris Askham

Leave Her Alone
Illustrated by Chris Askham

Secrets
Illustrated by Chris Askham

Sleepover
Illustrated by Chris Askham

Don't Do It!
Illustrated by Chris Askham